Helium Resources of the United States - 2001

Technical Note 408

December 2001

By:

B.D. Gage
D.L. Driskill

U.S. Department of the Interior

Bureau of Land Management

Unit of Measure Abbreviation
Used in Report

Bcf	billion cubic feet
Btu	British thermal unit
°F	degree Fahrenheit
MMcf	million cubic feet
%	percent
psia	pounds per square inch, absolute
Tcf	trillion cubic feet

Suggested citation:

Gage, B.D. and D.L. Driskill. 2001. Helium resources of the United States—2001, Technical Note 408. Bureau of Land Management. Denver, Colorado. BLM/NM/ST-02/001+3700. 30 pp.

Table of Contents

Figures

Tables

Helium Resources of the United States—2001

By Brent D. Gage[1] and David L. Driskill[2]

Abstract

This report differs from past reports in defining helium reserves in that it includes only the estimated helium contained in fields and formations from which helium is currently being recovered. Previous reports had placed nondepleting fields and formations into the helium reserve category.

The identified helium resources of the United States are estimated at 468 Bcf, as of December 31, 2000. This includes 144 Bcf of demonstrated reserves, 137 Bcf of demonstrated marginal reserves, and 37 Bcf of demonstrated subeconomic resources. The identified resources also include 150 Bcf of helium in inferred subeconomic resources. The demonstrated helium resources contained on Federal lands are approximately 155 Bcf, including 30 Bcf in underground storage in the Cliffside Gasfield near Amarillo, Texas. In addition to the identified helium resources, undiscovered helium resources in the United States are estimated at a most likely volume of 110 Bcf, with a maximum volume of 254 Bcf and a minimum volume of 45 Bcf. Also reported are 53 Bcf of helium in nonconventional and low helium content natural gases.

Current extraction of helium in the United States occurs mainly from natural gases produced from the Hugoton gas area in Kansas, Oklahoma, and Texas, and the Riley Ridge area in southwestern Wyoming. Helium sales in the United States in 2000 was approximately 4.5 Bcf, with 3.5 Bcf extracted from natural gas and 1.0 Bcf from crude helium storage at the Cliffside Gasfield. The volume of helium produced with the natural gas in the Hugoton area continues to decline. The current trend at the Cliffside Gasfield is the withdrawal of privately owned crude helium by private industry.

The growth of helium sales was about 330 MMcf from 1999 to 2000. This trend is expected to continue over the next 3 to 4 years with exploitation of other sources of helium expected in 2004 and 2005. The pure plants currently located along the Government's pipeline will reach maximum helium production capacity at about this time. If the growth of sales continues to increase at about 300 MMcf per year and helium extraction from natural gas in the midcontinent declines at 10 percent annually, the expected helium projects will help slow the growth of withdrawal from the Cliffside Gasfield.

[1]Petroleum Engineer, Bureau of Land Management, Helium Operations, Amarillo, Texas
[2]Geologist, Bureau of Land Management, Helium Operations, Amarillo, Texas

Introduction

The identified helium resources of the United States are estimated at 468 Bcf[3]. This includes both demonstrated (measured and indicated) and inferred helium contained in proved, probable, and possible natural gas resources[4]. It also includes helium previously separated from natural gases and stored at the Cliffside Gasfield in Potter County, Texas. Helium contained in other occurrences of natural gas in the United States is estimated at 53 Bcf; this includes helium in nonconventional gas reserves and low helium content natural gas. The undiscovered helium resources in the United States are estimated at a most likely value of 110 Bcf. This results in a total helium resource base of 631 Bcf.

This publication is the 12th in a series of reports on the helium resources of the Nation. The first of these reports gave information on helium resources as of January 1, 1973 (1)[5]. The reports have been published approximately every 2 years with the last reporting information as of December 31, 1996 (2-11). It has been 3 years since the last update to this publication. During this period, demand for helium has exceeded supply leading to withdrawal from the Cliffside Gasfield.

The Helium Operations Office has been estimating the Nation's helium resources for about 55 years in connection with a search for helium occurrences that has been conducted for over 80 years. These activities are carried on: (1) to ensure a continuing supply of helium to fill essential Federal needs, (2) to provide information to the Secretary of the Interior so that helium resources reserved to the United States on Federal land can be properly managed, and (3) to provide the public with information on a limited natural resource that is being depleted.

The Mineral Lands Leasing Act of 1920 reserves to the United States all helium found on Federal lands leased under the provisions of that Act. The responsibility for ensuring a supply of helium to meet essential Federal needs was assigned to the Secretary of the Interior by the Helium Act of March 31, 1925. This was followed by the Helium Act Amendments of 1960, which among other things allowed the Secretary of the Interior to purchase crude helium for storage at the Cliffside Field. The most recent legislation pertaining to helium is the Helium Privatization Act of 1996. The helium resource estimates and supply/demand forecasts presented in this report are realistic for the short term; however, as in all long term forecasts, less reliance should be placed on the estimates toward the end of the forecast.

The estimate of the total helium resource base of 631 Bcf is less than the 750 Bcf estimated as of December 31, 1996. The decrease is due to changes in estimates of natural gas resources by the Potential Gas Committee (PGC) (12). The identified resources are classified based on degree of geological assurance of occurrence. This classification results in the categories termed measured, indicated, and inferred. See the Glossary for definitions of these terms and their relationship to the oil and gas industry terms of proved, probable, and possible. Measured resources, including storage, are 208 Bcf; indicated resources are 110 Bcf; and inferred resources are 150 Bcf.

---

[3]All values in this report, unless otherwise stated, are at 14.65 psia and 60 °F as of December 31, 2000.
[4]See Glossary for definitions of resource terms. The definitions and uses of the terms in this report follow the general guidelines established by the United States Geological Survey (USGS) as published in USGS Bulletin 1450-A, *Principles of the Mineral Resource Classification System of the United States Bureau of Mines and the United States Geological Survey, 1976*, and later revised in Geological Circular 831, 1980.
[5] The numbers in parentheses refer to items in the References section near the end of this report.

The identified helium resources can be subdivided into three categories (Figure1): (1) reserves containing 144 Bcf, which includes helium in underground storage; (2) marginal reserves containing 137 Bcf; and (3) subeconomic resources containing 187 Bcf. The helium resource base also includes approximately 53 Bcf of helium in other natural gas occurrences. These natural gas occurrences include coalbed methane and natural gases with very low helium contents, generally less than 0.05 percent. The undiscovered helium resources comprise the remainder of the helium resource base, and the estimate of 110 Bcf is based on the most likely speculative gas resource values provided by the PGC. The minimum value for the undiscovered resources is 45 Bcf and the maximum value is 254 Bcf. Definitions for these and other helium and natural gas resource terms are found in the Glossary.

This report categorizes the resources on an economic basis. The helium content of the gases is an economic consideration because the extraction costs generally decrease as helium content increases. However, other factors that affect the economic potential of helium deposits are also considered and included in classifying the helium resources. These factors include the average daily rate of processed gas, hydrocarbon recovery, life of the reserves, size of reserves, and proximity to the Government's helium storage system.

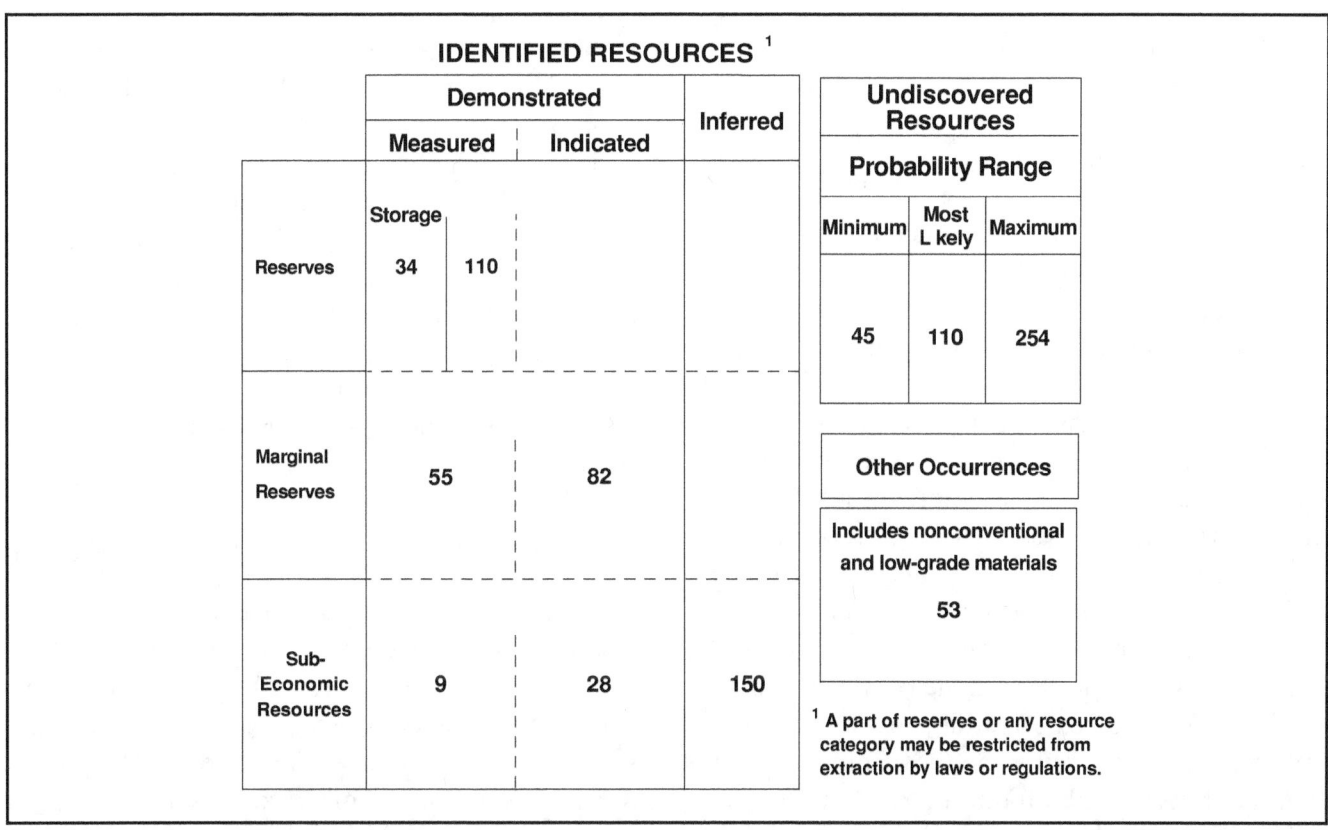

Figure 1. Identified and undiscovered helium resources in the United States (billion cubic feet at 14.65 psia and 60°F). Modified from *Principles of a Resource/Reserve Classification of Minerals* (Geological Survey Circular 831, 1980).

Identified Helium Resources

Helium occurs as a constituent of natural gas, which is presently the only economical source. Helium is also present in the atmosphere, but for the purposes of this report, is not considered as part of the helium resource base. The natural gas in which helium is found may be normal fuel gas; naturally occurring, low-Btu gas; or nonconventional gas resources such as coalbed methane and carbon dioxide gas. The helium content of natural gas resources is derived from Bureau records of helium analyses of natural gas samples, which are a part of the Bureau's resource database. The analysis of natural gas and limited evaluations of helium resources started in 1917. Over 20,600 natural gas samples from wells and pipelines in the United States and other countries have been analyzed through 2000 and 16,058 of these analyses have been documented in 42 Bureau publications. These publications are listed in the bibliography of this report.

Helium in Storage

In 1961, the Government contracted to purchase helium from five extraction plants built by four private companies adjacent to large natural gas transmission pipelines. The gas, principally from the West Panhandle and Hugoton gasfields in the Oklahoma and Texas Panhandles and in southwestern Kansas, was being produced for fuel. As the gas was burned, the helium was released to the atmosphere and wasted. Using private funds, these companies constructed plants to extract crude helium for sale to the Government. The helium was delivered into a Government owned pipeline that connected all plants with the Bush Dome in the Cliffside Gasfield near Amarillo, Texas. Further information concerning the Government's helium purchases can be found in the first report of this series (1) and the section in this report on the history and uses of helium.

Bush Dome was the source of helium-bearing natural gas that was produced for helium extraction at the Government's Amarillo Helium Plant from 1929 until the plant ceased helium extraction operations in April 1970. About 110 Bcf of natural gas has been produced from the Cliffside Gasfield and there are about 200 Bcf of remaining recoverable gas reserves. The natural gas averages about 1.86 percent contained helium; therefore, the remaining native helium reserves are about 3.7 Bcf. Since the Amarillo Helium Plant ceased helium extraction operations, natural gas has been produced from Bush Dome for fuel gas and helium extraction at the Government's Exell Helium Plant operations north of Amarillo, Texas.

The Helium Privatization Act of 1996 mandated cessation of the operation of the Exell Helium Plant, with private industry supplying Federal agencies using In-Kind Crude Helium Sales (IKCHS) contracts. Helium contained in the remaining native gas is included with the helium in the measured helium reserves. As of December 31, 2000, the helium stored in Bush Dome totaled 33.7 Bcf. Of this total, 29.6 Bcf was accepted by the Government from the conservation plants under contract and was excess to Federal market demands. The other 4.1 Bcf is stored by the Government for private companies under separate storage contracts.

Other Measured Helium Resources

The demonstrated, measured helium reserves and resources are considered the most accurate estimates of this report and are 174 Bcf, not including storage and other occurrences of helium. The measured helium is subdivided into reserves, marginal reserves, and subeconomic resources. Presently, all measured reserves are in helium-rich natural gas. The marginal reserves and subeconomic helium resources are contained in both helium-rich and helium-lean natural gas. All gasfields known to contain at least 0.05 percent helium have been individually evaluated and are part of the demonstrated helium resources. Fields containing less than 0.05 percent helium are not individually evaluated. The helium resources in these fields are estimated by using average helium contents of natural gas from representative fields and basins and applying those values to the Department of Energy/Energy Information Administration (DOE/EIA) reserve estimates (13). These helium resources, although they are contained in proved natural gas reserves, are reported as other occurrences of helium.

Measured Helium Reserves

Measured helium reserves are estimated at 110 Bcf, excluding storage. These reserves are located in eight gas-producing areas in six States. The reserves by State and area are listed in Table 1. Locations are shown in Figure 2.

Since 1950, the Bureau has been making estimates of the helium resources of the Nation. For several years, the estimates included only the fields that contained major deposits of at least 0.30 percent helium. These fields were the Hugoton in southwestern Kansas and the Oklahoma and Texas Panhandles, the West Panhandle in Texas, the Greenwood in Kansas, the Keyes in Oklahoma, and the Cliffside in Texas. Even today these fields are estimated to contain approximately 32 percent, or 35 Bcf, of the measured helium reserves. The natural gas from all these fields is being produced for fuel, and the helium that is not extracted is lost to the atmosphere as the natural gas is burned.

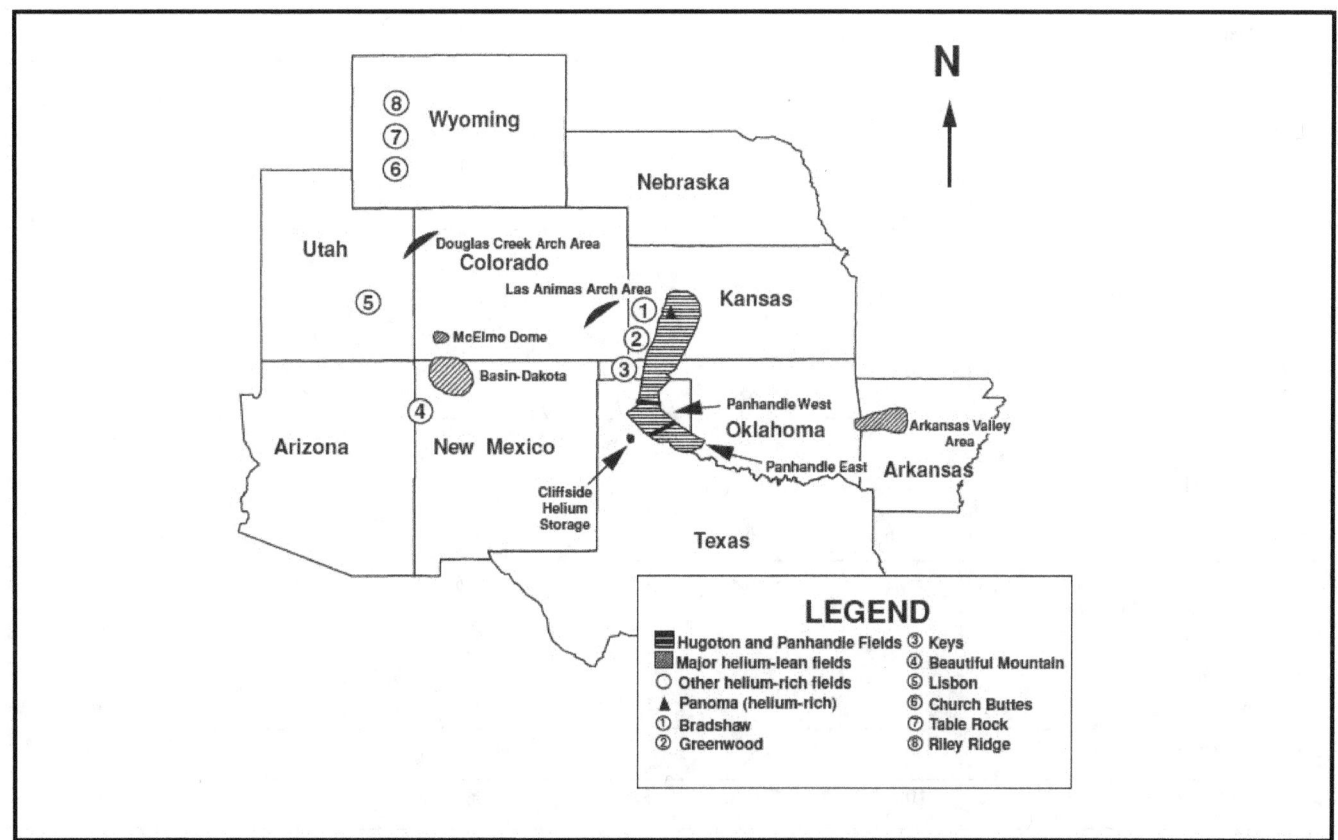

Figure 2. Location of major helium-bearing gasfields.

Table 1. Measured helium reserves. Volumes are in MMcf as of December 31, 2000.

State	Area	Helium Reserves	Federally Owned	Marginal Helium Reserves	Federally Owned	Subeconomic Helium Resources	Federally Owned
Arizona	Apache County			998	0		
Arkansas	Arkansas Valley					956	73
Colorado	Baca County			173	5		
	Douglas Crk Arch			368	355		
	Paradox Basin					4,389	3,388
	Miscellaneous			308	219	64	64
	Las Animas Arch	1,093	0				
Total Colorado		1,093	0	849	579	4,453	3,452
Kansas	Hugoton	32,397	1,111				
	Other Areas			407	0	525	22
Total Kansas		32,397	1,111	407	0	525	22
Montana	Rudyard/Utopia			189	0		
	Other Areas					936	139
New Mexico	Chaves County			1,717	1,082		
	Northwest NM			679	24		
Total New Mexico				2,396	1,106		
Oklahoma	Guymon Hugoton	2,079	12				
	Keyes Gas Area	456	6				
	Other Areas					947	3
Total Oklahoma		2,535	18			947	3
Texas	Cliffside Area Native Gas	3,719	3,719				
	District 10	6,682	18				
	Other Areas					1,062	5
Total Texas		10,401	3,737			1,062	5
Utah	Lisbon Area	651	589				
	Other Areas			1,135	934	155	94
Total Utah		651	589	1,135	934	155	94
Wyoming	Riley Ridge	63,510	59,128	46,923	43,906		
	Church Buttes Area			1,587	773		
	Washakie Basin			1,033	700	368	151
Total Wyoming		63,510	59,128	49,543	45,379	368	151
Miscellaneous States						51	0
Total United States		**110,587**	**64,583**	**55,517**	**47,988**	**9,453**	**3,939**

As the helium resources evaluation program in the United States progressed, more comprehensive data were collected and the estimates improved. In 1961, a major improvement in the program took place. For the first time, helium reserves were estimated for all fields in the United States from which samples containing more than 0.30 percent helium had been analyzed in connection with the gas-sampling program. Available data for many of these smaller fields were limited for the first evaluation efforts; however, over the intervening years, data has been collected from all known, available sources. This has resulted in a comprehensive assessment of the total helium resources of the country.

Before the implementation of crude helium purchases in late 1962, all of the previously mentioned gasfields with large helium reserves were being produced for fuel. The resultant loss of helium amounted to approximately 8 Bcf per year. Under the crude helium purchase program, approximately 3.5 Bcf of helium, that otherwise would have been wasted, was saved annually from 1963 through November 12, 1973, when the Government purchase of helium from the private conservation plants ceased.

Some of the gasfields that contain measured reserves of helium are not being produced, and the helium is not being wasted. These are classified as nondepleting helium reserves. There are 38 fields in 7 States that are nondepleting. These nondepleting fields contain marginal reserves and subeconomic resources of helium. Table 2 lists the nondepleting and depleting resources by category.

There are various reasons why these fields are not being produced. Some are located in remote areas where pipeline connections are not presently available. In others, the gas is being used in pressure maintenance operations to produce associated oil. In the majority of these fields, however, the helium is in natural gas that has a low-heating value and thus is not suitable for fuel. Fields in the first two groups will be put on production eventually, and the helium reserves moved to the depleting category. For example, the Lisbon Field in southeastern Utah had been under pressure maintenance and secondary recovery operations since 1969, when gas production operations began. In conjunction with the gas production, helium extraction capabilities were added and helium recovery began during 1994. As natural

Table 2. Depleting and nondepleting demonstrated helium reserves and resources. Volumes in Bcf at 14.65 psia and 60°F.

	Depleting	Federal	Nondepleting	Federal
Measured Reserves[1]	110	65	<1	0
Indicated Reserves	0	0	0	0
Measured Marginal Reserves	3	2	52	46
Indicated Marginal Reserves	76	<1	6	3
Measured Subeconomic	8	4	1	<1
Indicated Subeconomic	28	<1	0	0
Total	225	71	59	49

[1]Does not include 34 Bcf in storage, of which 30 Bcf is owned by the Government.

gas prices rise, some of the fields with low-heating value gas will be produced. In 1986, one major field in this group, Riley Ridge in Sublette County, Wyoming, began production from the Madison Formation. This transferred approximately 71 Bcf of helium from the nondepleting to the depleting category of measured helium reserves.

The Mineral Lands Leasing Act of 1920 reserves to the United States all helium found on Federal lands leased under the provisions of that Act. In this report, the term "Federal lands" applies to those lands on which the Government owns the gas rights. Under these provisions, the United States is estimated to own 95 Bcf of helium found in measured helium reserves on Federal lands. The measured helium reserves are comprised of 95 Bcf of depleting reserves (see Table 2).

Measured Marginal Helium Reserves

The measured marginal helium reserves are approximately 55 Bcf. These marginal reserves are found in 12 gas-producing areas in 7 states (see Table 1). A portion of these marginal helium reserves are found in different geologic formations in fields also containing measured helium reserves or in proximity to these reserves. They are classified as marginal helium reserves primarily based on the expectation that an improvement in economics may result in extraction of helium. (See Appendix A, Guidelines for Determining Helium Reserves and Resources.)

Helium-rich gasfields account for all of the measured marginal helium reserves. These resources are classified as marginal reserves because of their small size, generally less than 0.5 Bcf of helium. In the future, it is possible that helium may be extracted from these formations.

Measured Subeconomic Helium Resources

This category is made up of both helium-rich and helium-lean gasfields. Each helium-rich gasfield containing less than 150 MMcf of helium, and each helium-lean gasfield containing more than 150 MMcf and less than 1 Bcf of helium is included. One exception is McElmo Dome in southwestern Colorado, which contains approximately 5 Bcf of helium. The gas composition in McElmo Dome is mainly carbon dioxide with a helium content of 0.07 percent, making it unlikely that helium will ever be extracted. The measured subeconomic helium resources are estimated at approximately 9 Bcf. Nearly all of these resources are depleting and most are in helium-lean gasfields, with less than 0.5 Bcf in helium-rich gasfields. The helium resources are listed by State in Table 1. Although it is possible to extract helium from gasfields in this category, it is unlikely. These gasfields are isolated from current helium extraction facilities and contain small amounts of helium.

The Arkansas Valley Area was moved from marginal reserves to subeconomic resources. Gas samples from various zones of Pennsylvanian age from many of these fields have been analyzed by the Bureau. These analyses show similar gas and helium contents with very little variation. The economics of extracting helium from the Arkansas Valley area will be a function of helium prices and revenue derived from the extraction and sale of other constituents of the gas stream. The economics may never favor extraction of helium in this area.

Indicated Helium Resources

Indicated helium resources of the United States are 82 Bcf of marginal reserves and 28 Bcf in subeconomic resources. The indicated helium resources are derived from the PGC's estimate of probable resources of natural gas. The average helium contents are estimated for each PGC region or basin and used to determine the amount of indicated helium in each basin. See Figure 3 for a general map of PGC regions. The assumption is that probable gas resources in a basin will contain similar gases and helium content as proven gas reserves. However, new discoveries may contain significantly higher helium content than previously found in a particular basin. In addition, some basins contain indicated helium that has been evaluated in conjunction with individual gasfield evaluations. This helium is included as part of the PGC-derived value, not added to it, except low-Btu gases that are not included in the PGC's estimate.

There are no indicated helium reserves carried in the helium reserves category.

The indicated marginal helium reserves contain 76 Bcf of depleting helium and 6 Bcf of nondepleting helium[6]. Only about 3 Bcf of this is known to be on Federal land. The indicated subeconomic resources are all in depleting reservoirs and less than 1 Bcf is known to be on Federal land.

Approximately 7 Bcf of the indicated helium is associated with individually evaluated gasfields. Of this, 6 Bcf is contained in marginal helium reserves and 1 Bcf is contained in subeconomic resources. The remaining 103 Bcf of the indicated

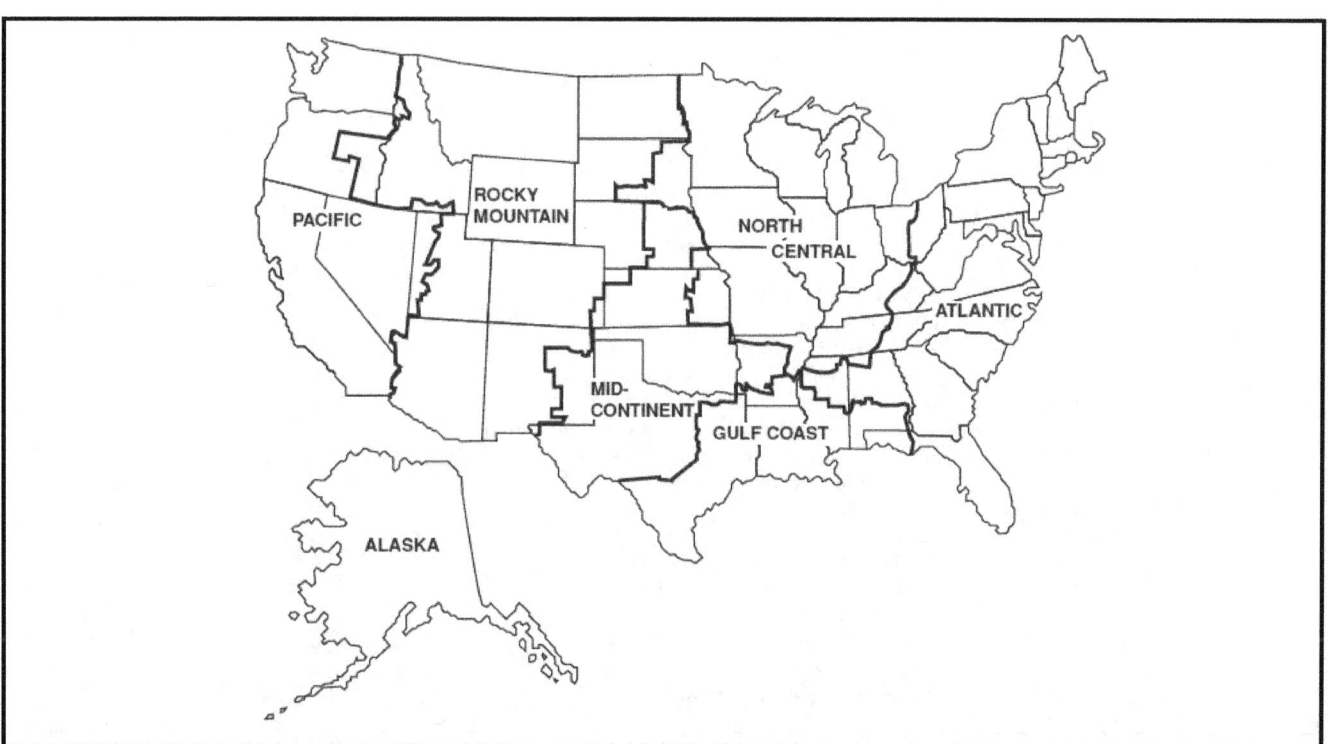

Figure 3. Map of Potential Gas Committee (PGC) regions.

---

[6] Technically, all indicated helium is nondepleting since these resources are not developed or actually producing. Terms "depleting" and "nondepleting" as used here show that the helium is associated with currently depleting or nondepleting fields.

Table 3. Estimated average helium contents of gas resources by PGC region and basin.

Region and Basin			Avg. Helium Content	Footnotes
Alaska			0.0111%	1
Atlantic:	P-100	New England and Adirondack Uplifts	0.0233%	1
	P-110	Atlantic Coastal Basin	0.0233%	1
	P-120	Appalachian Basin	0.0497%	1
	P-130	Piedmont-Blue Ridge Province	0.0497%	1
	P-140	South Georgia-Peninsular Florida	0.0150%	1
	P-150	Black Warrior Basin	0.0100%	1
Gulf Coast:	P-300	Louisiana-Mississippi-Alabama Salt Dome	0.0430%	1
	P-310	Louisiana Gulf Coast Basin	0.0020%	1
	P-320	East Texas Basin	0.0017%	1
	P-330	Texas Gulf Coast Basin	0.0020%	1
	P-930	Eastern Gulf Shelf	0.0014%	2
	P-931	Eastern Gulf Slope	0.0014%	1
	P-935	Louisiana Shelf	0.0014%	2
	P-936	Louisiana Slope	0.0014%	2
	P-940	Texas Shelf	0.0014%	2
	P-941	Texas Slope	0.0014%	2
	P-945	Gulf of Mexico Outer Continental Slope	0.0014%	1
Midcontinent:	P-400	Central Kansas Uplift, Salina Basin	0.2081%	1
	P-410	Arkoma Basin	0.0110%	1
	P-420	Anadarko, Palo Duro Basins, etc.	0.2081%	1
	P-430	Fort Worth and Strawn Basins, Bend Arch	0.2550%	1
	P-440	Permian Basin	0.0282%	1
North Central			0.0371%	1
Pacific			0.0069%	1
Rocky Mountain:	P-500	Williston Basin	0.0802%	1
	P-510	Powder River Basin	0.0793%	1
	P-515	Big Horn Basin	0.0490%	1
	P-520	Wind River Basin	0.0417%	1
	P-530	Greater Green River Basin < 15,000 ft	0.0760%	1
	P-530	Greater Green River Basin > 15,000 ft	0.5190%	3
	P-535	Denver Basin, Chadron Arch and Las Animas Arch	0.0642%	1
	P-540	Uinta/Piceance Basins; Park and Eagle Basins	0.1720%	1
	P-545	San Juan Mountains; San Louis and Raton Basins	0.0230%	2
	P-550	Paradox Basin	0.4150%	1
	P-555	San Juan Basin	0.0228%	1
	P-560	Southern Basin and Range Province	0.0150%	2
	P-565	Plateau Province, Black Mesa Basin	0.0070%	2
	P-570	Sweetgrass Arch	0.1602%	1
	P-575	Montana Folded Belt	0.1602%	1
	P-580	Snake River Basin	0.0275%	1
	P-590	Wyoming-Utah-Idaho Thrust Belt	0.0824%	2

FOOTNOTES:

1. The average helium content is weighted based on the number of gas samples from each formation and field combination in the region.

2. The average helium content is derived from pipeline gas surveys carried out by the Bureau and is weighted based on gas volumes flowing through gas plants in the region.

3. The average helium content is weighted heavily to the high helium-bearing gas in the Riley Ridge field. The helium contents of other gases in the area also are considered.

Table 4. Estimated indicated helium resources by PGC basin. All volumes are in Bcf at 14.65 psia and 60°F.

PGC Basin		Reserves	Marginal Reserves	Subeconomic Resources
P-530	Greater Green River Basin >15,000'			
P-550	Paradox Basin		2.09	
P-400	Central Kansas Uplift, Salina Basin		0.32	
P-420	Anadarko, Palo Duro Basins, etc.		47.83	
P-430	Ft. Worth and Strawn Basins, Bend Arch			7.37
P-540	Uinta, Piceance Basins		25.44	
P-570	Sweetgrass Arch			0.71
P-120	Appalachian Basin			9.87
P-500	Williston Basin			0.60
P-510	Powder River Basin			1.14
P-515	Big Horn Basin			0.41
P-530	Greater Green River Basin<15,000'			6.88
P-535	Denver Basin, Chadron Arch			0.85
P-590	Wyoming-Utah-Idaho Thrust Belt			0.66
	Total	0	75.68	28.49

resources is derived from the PGC's probable gas resources estimates. Because more importance is placed on reserves and marginal reserves, only gasfields containing helium reserves and marginal helium reserves are individually evaluated for indicated resources. In the subeconomic category, all indicated resource estimates are derived from the PGC probable gas resource values.

Table 3 shows the average helium contents by PGC basin as projected by the Bureau. The estimated indicated helium resources for each PGC basin have been placed in a resource category based on size and helium content. The same criteria used in determining resource placement for the measured reserves are applied to the indicated resources. These resource estimates are shown in Table 4.

Inferred Helium Resources

The inferred helium resources of the United States are 150 Bcf in subeconomic resources. The inferred helium resources are derived from the PGC's estimate of possible gas resources. As with indicated helium resources, estimates are made of the average helium contents of the possible gas resources for the PGC areas and basins. The average helium contents are based on the helium contents of proven reserves and all areas that have potential for significant helium finds in the future. Every basin and area studied, with the exception of the Gulf Coast and Pacific areas, have contained some helium-rich natural gas. Possible Federal ownership of the inferred resources was not estimated. Table 5 shows the estimated inferred helium resources for each PGC basin and the category in which the resources are placed.

The PGC's possible gas resources are placed in the subeconomic category. Probable resources are based on extension of productive fields and are more certain than the possible gas resources. Possible resources are a less assured supply because they are postulated to exist outside known fields, but are associated with a productive formation in a productive province. Possible resources are accounted for in Figure 1 under inferred subeconomic resources. The PGC possible resources will be updated as more information becomes available on the basins. For this reason, less reliance should be put on the helium resources of these areas until gas production is proven by development of new fields. Although we have helium contents for fields in the areas covered by the PGC, it is difficult to assign anything other than subeconomic to the postulated resources. This is done to keep from skewing the extent of helium associated with these new fields.

Table 5. Estimated inferred helium resources by PGC basin. All volumes are in Bcf at 14.65 psia and 60°F.

PGC	Basin or Region	Reserves	Marginal Reserves	Subeconomic Resources
P-530	Greater Green River Basin>15,000'			29.72
P-550	Paradox Basin			4.17
P-400	Central Kansas Uplift, Salina Basin			0.74
P-420	Anadarko, Palo Duro Basins, etc.			42.84
P-430	Ft. Worth and Strawn Basins, Bend Arch			1.76
P-540	Uinta, Piceance Basins			27.32
P-570	Sweetgrass Arch			1.53
P-575	Montana Folded Belt			6.44
	Alaska			1.83
P-120	Appalachian Basin			3.65
P-150	Black Warrior Basin			0.07
	Gulf Coast Region (on and offshore)			4.34
P-410	Arkoma Basin			0.20
P-440	Permian Basin			6.54
	North Central Region			3.79
	Pacific Region			1.55
P-500	Williston Basin			0.81
P-510	Powder River Basin			1.72
P-515	Big Horn Basin			0.56
P-520	Wind River Basin			3.57
P-530	Greater Green River Basin <15,000'			3.71
P-535	Denver Basin, Chadron Arch			0.78
P-545	San Juan Mtns, San Louis/Raton Basin			0.09
P-555	San Juan Basin			1.61
P-560	Southern Basin and Range Province			0.21
P-590	Wyoming-Utah-Idaho Thrust Belt			0.83
	Total	0	0	150.38

Other Helium Occurrences

Other occurrences of helium include helium contained in nonconventional natural gas and extremely lean (low-grade) helium occurrences. All proven reserves of natural gas that contain less than 0.05 percent helium are in this category. In addition, helium in coalbed methane and some carbon dioxide occurrences are also included. The helium resources in other occurrences are about 53 Bcf.

An average helium content is applied to the DOE/EIA reserves of natural gas, less the evaluated natural gasfields containing measured helium, to arrive at a value for helium contained in the remaining gas reserves. The average helium contents are derived from the helium survey analyses of gas wells and the continuing survey of gas transmission pipelines and are weighted based on flow through the pipelines. The total helium in other occurrences from this source is about 30 Bcf.

Also part of the other occurrences of helium are the coalbed methane resources and some carbon dioxide resources. The Bureau has estimated that this methane contains about 6 Bcf of helium. There are other coalbed methane areas being developed and the PGC is estimating natural gas resources for their regions. Other coalbed methane projects being worked on will be integrated into this study as more information becomes available. The helium resources in the carbon dioxide gases of the Sheep Mountain area of Colorado are less than 1 Bcf. Other carbon dioxide producing fields have significant helium contents and are categorized as helium reserves, marginal reserves (Riley Ridge Field–nondepleting formations), and subeconomic resources (McElmo Dome) as previously discussed.

Additionally, certain evaluated fields containing helium-lean natural gas are contained in this category. These fields generally contain small amounts of helium and are remote from major gas transmission lines. These miscellaneous fields contain about 3 Bcf of helium.

The last source of helium in this category is from certain estimates for the resource category designated as probable gas resources (indicated) by the PGC (Table 4). Basins and areas that contain probable gas resources with average helium contents of less than 0.05 percent are also placed in the other occurrences category and contain approximately 14 Bcf of helium. Table 6 lists all estimates of helium in other occurrences.

Table 6. Estimated helium in other occurrences. Volumes in Bcf at 14.65 psia and 60°F.

Category	Occurrence
Coalbed methane	
Black Warrior Basin	5.74
CO_2 Resources	
Colorado/New Mexico	0.74
DOE/EIA	29.60
Miscellaneous	2.90
From PGC-Probable:	
Alaska	3.44
P-150 Black Warrior Basin	0.05
Gulf Coast Region	2.89
P-410 Arkoma Basin	0.24
P-440 Permian Basin	2.64
North Central Region	0.90
Pacific Region	0.24
P-520 Wind River Basin	1.90
P-555 San Juan Basin	1.33
Total	52.61

Undiscovered Helium Resources

The undiscovered helium resources in the United States are estimated at a most likely value of 110 Bcf, with a minimum value of 45 Bcf, and a maximum value of 254 Bcf. The estimates are based on the PGC's minimum most likely and maximum speculative gas resources combined with the Bureau's estimate of average helium contents. The same average helium contents that are used for indicated and inferred helium resources are used for undiscovered resources. No attempt was made to estimate the minimum and maximum helium contents because, for most basins, the helium contents fall within a very narrow range of values. For example, analyses of gases from the offshore Gulf Coast area have never indicated helium contents greater than 0.05 percent. In areas such as the midcontinent, where the helium contents have a wider range of values, statistical analyses showed no pattern to the helium contents based on size of reservoir or discovery. Further, studies of proven gas reserves by basin, reservoir, and helium contents (14) show that gases in most basins and reservoirs contain helium contents within a narrow range of values. Also, new discoveries within these basins tend to follow the helium content pattern of past discoveries.

Production and Extraction

Background

The Bureau's role in helium dates to World War I when the Army and Navy became interested in using helium as an inert lifting gas and contacted the Bureau for assistance because of its natural gas expertise. The Helium Act of 1925 officially placed the helium program under Bureau control. The Bureau built a large-scale helium extraction and purification facility and began operations in 1929. During World War II, demand increased significantly and four more small government plants were built.

Increased helium demand in the 1950s led to construction of the Keyes, Oklahoma, helium plant in 1959. Dwindling midcontinent natural gas supplies aroused concerns that no economic source of helium would exist by the turn of the century and led to the passage of amendments to the Helium Act of 1925. The Helium Act Amendments of 1960 provided for the conservation of helium for essential Government needs and also was intended to promote the development of a private helium industry. The Act directed the Secretary of the Interior to purchase and store helium for future use and to maintain helium production and purification plants and related helium storage, transmission, and shipping facilities.

Purchases for the conservation program were made from private companies, which added crude helium extraction plants to existing gas processing facilities. The Bureau built a high-pressure pipeline to transport the helium from Bushton, Kansas, and intermediate points to the Bureau-owned Cliffside Gasfield for storage. In 1973, the contracts with private companies were canceled because the Secretary determined that the long-term needs of the Government were adequately fulfilled. In the mid-1970s, the Bureau began accepting privately owned crude helium for storage at the Cliffside Gasfield. As of December 31, 2000, private industry had about 4.1 Bcf of helium stored at Cliffside.

Helium Privatization Act of 1996

On October 9, 1996, the President signed the Helium Privatization Act of 1996 (Public Law 104-273). This legislation directed the Government to cease the production and sale of refined helium on April 9, 1998. Some of the remaining key components of this legislation are as follows:

- The disposal of all helium production, refining, and sales related assets not later than 24 months after the closure of the helium refinery.

Status: An historical review was initiated in June 1999, and reports were completed in August 1999. The Phase 1 environmental site assessment was initiated in early 1999, and reports were completed in July 1999. The National Park Service is currently preparing an Historic Architectural Engineering Report on the Amarillo and Exell Plants. Additionally, an application has been filed with the Texas Voluntary Compliance Program for the Landis Property and a contractor has been secured for sampling and assessment. Property disposal actions continue.

- Offer for sale the Federal reserves of crude helium in excess of 600 MMcf to begin no later than January 1, 2005, and complete sales by January 1, 2015.

Status: Crude helium sales (in-kind) for helium that is sold to Federal agencies and their contractors by private companies began in January 1998. The in-kind crude-helium sales were 227 MMcf in 2000. Open market sales of the crude helium was reviewed in a legislatively mandated study conducted by the National Academy of Sciences (NAS) concerning the impact on national, scientific, and military interests. The NAS study was completed in March 2000. Helium regulations, however, are currently being developed and, once in place, will be used to guide open market sales of the crude helium.

- Continue operation of the helium storage field and conservation pipeline for storage and distribution of crude helium. This component is to meet private industry and Government needs using IKCHS contracts with private suppliers.

- Continue the collection of helium royalty and fee sales for helium extracted from Federal lands.

- Continue helium resource evaluation and reserve tracking to monitor helium availability for essential Government programs.

Uses of Helium

Helium is chemically inert, which means that no other element will combine with helium at any temperature or pressure. Helium is the second lightest element, with hydrogen being the lightest. Helium liquifies at approximately -452°F, making it useful in cryogenics, the study of the behavior of matter and energy at temperatures below -270°F. The properties possessed by helium make it an element that can be used in a variety of applications.

Since helium will not burn or react with other substances, it is used to shield reactive metals, such as aluminum, from contamination by other elements during arc welding. The inert characteristics of helium keep it from reacting in the body, which allows it to be used in breathing mixtures supplied to some undersea explorers and operating-room patients. Helium is seven times lighter than air and nonexplosive, thus making it applicable as the lifting gas inside high-altitude weather and research balloons and lighter-than-air craft.

Helium is used to control atmospheric conditions in special chambers where silicon crystals used in electronic applications are grown. The production of fiber-optic wire requires an ultrapure inert atmosphere. Helium's immunity to radioactivity led to its use as a heat transfer medium in gas-cooled nuclear power reactors. The molecular size of helium allows it to escape through the tiniest holes, which makes helium useful for detecting leaks during the manufacture of sealed fluid systems like those used in refrigerators and vacuum systems. The very low temperature at which helium liquifies causes certain metals to become superconductors, losing all resistance to the flow of electricity. This has made possible the construction of powerful magnets that can be used to monitor physical and chemical conditions inside the human body, and to accelerate subatomic particles to velocities near the speed of light for experiments in high-energy physics.

The development of liquid-fueled rockets increased the uses for helium in space exploration and missile technology. The Atlas, Saturn V, and Space Shuttle have applied the technology developed for helium used in space travel. The fuel tanks of all these spacecraft are pressurized by helium to push the fuel into the pumps feeding the rocket engines and to provide pressure, enabling thin-walled tanks to resist collapse when empty. The Space Shuttle also uses helium in the orbital maneuvering system engines that enable the shuttle to change the shape and altitude of its orbit.

Other evolving technologies that require the unique properties of helium are: (1) metastable helium for energy storage, which involves raising helium electrons to an excited energy state and then stabilizing the atom there; (2) helium ion tumor treatment, where large inert particles are required; (3) liquid helium-cooled superconducting microswitches, called Josephson junctions, which are much faster than conventional semiconductors and use less power; and (4) "aneutronic" nuclear fusion of deuterium and helium-3, which results in few or no neutrons. Figure 4 shows the uses of helium in 2000.

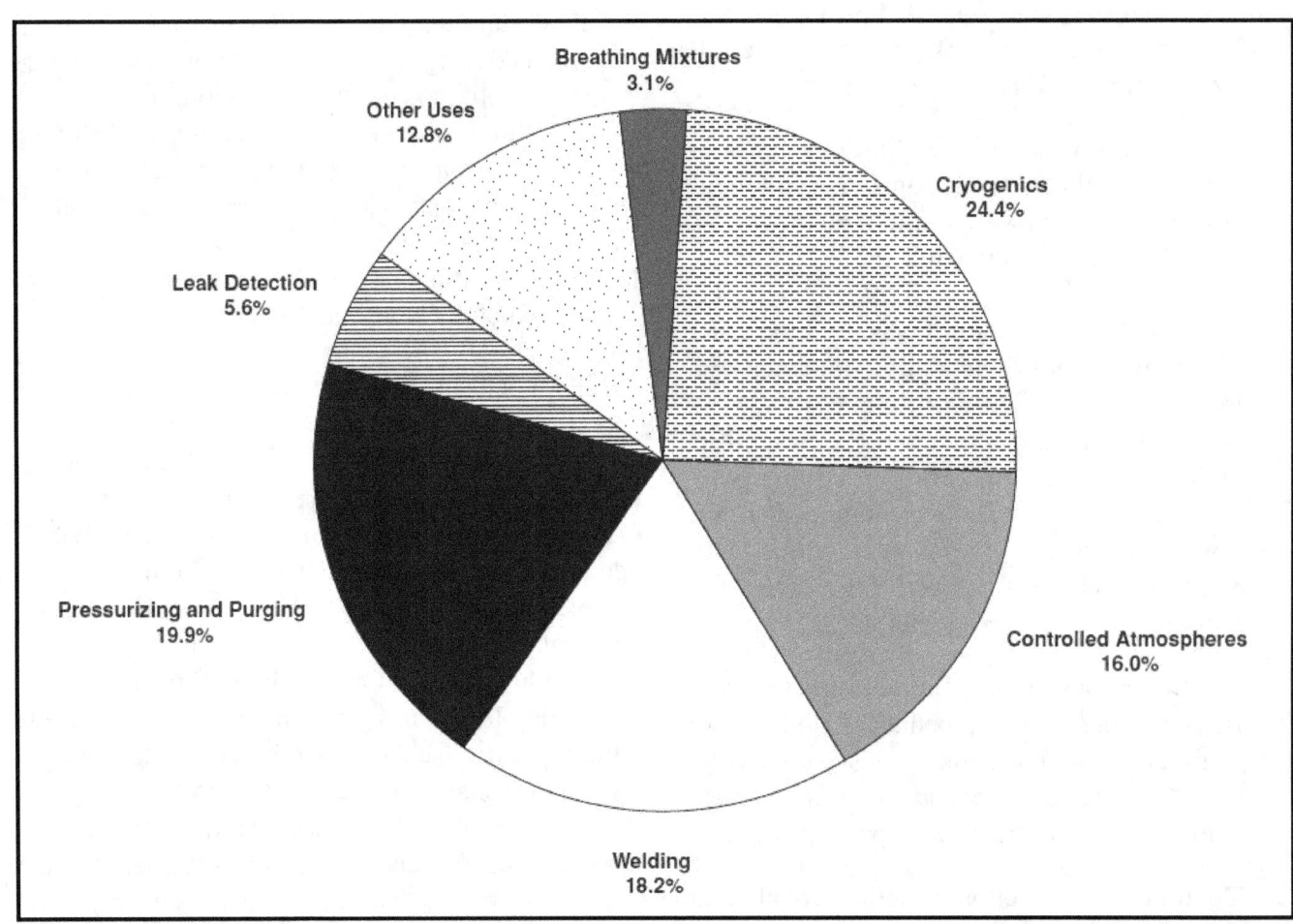

Figure 4. Uses of helium in 2000.

Contact with Private Companies

The Bureau sent letters to pure helium producers, crude-helium producers, and a representative sample of well operators in the midcontinent area. This was intended to gain a perspective of the current events taking place and any expected events that may affect the future of the helium market. There were a total of 18 letters sent to various companies of which only eight were answered. A solicitation of all the well operators was not undertaken, but the information received was from substantial operators in the area. The information obtained is presented below in generalized form.

Pure Helium

❏ There are pure helium extraction plans that would provide additional helium production of about 1.2 Bcf per year, if the liquifiers are operated at capacity. However, these projects will probably not be completed before 2004–2005. This extraction would occur at locations outside the United States.

❏ Other projects are also being considered for locations outside the United States. One of these could add an additional 0.6 Bcf, or more, of annual helium production. This is considered to be a longer term project. Two other projects are being considered, but the exact timeline, project talks, possibility of actual helium extraction, or quantities of helium extractable are not known.

❏ There are also projects being considered in the United States. There are four areas currently being considered for smaller scale production plants, but details are not certain at this time. There is an additional project being considered, which may produce 0.5 Bcf of helium annually. This project is being considered as this report is prepared for publication, but if the project is undertaken, the earliest expected date of helium production would be 2004–2005.

Crude Helium

❏ The expectations of additional crude-helium extraction are not as clearly defined as for pure helium. A new crude-helium plant should be coming on line by the end of 2001. This plant will be taking natural gas from a plant that has previously extracted crude-helium and this gas stream will be combined with other gas streams previously not exploited for helium. The economics of crude-helium extraction, based on letter responses, appear to be favorable for the future.

Well Operators

❏ The decline in natural gas production from the Kansas Hugoton and Panoma Fields from 1999 to 2000 was about 14 to 15 percent. The projections of future declines expected in these fields were obtained from well operators, producing three decline ranges. The expected annual production decline ranged from 14 to 15 percent, 11 to 13 percent, and 6 to 8 percent. Although the Kansas Hugoton and Panoma Fields are not the only fields from which helium is extracted, they are a major source of helium. The Kansas Corporation Commission recently allowed wells to be produced on vacuum, on a case-by-case basis. This is not widespread at this time, but there are expectations by some of the respondents that additional compression will be added in the future. This is expected to increase the number of wells operating under vacuum. The Panhandle West Field is expected to decline at about 5 percent annually. There is an active drilling program taking place in the Panhandle West Field, and some of the wells are being completed at reservoir pressures approaching the original field reservoir pressure. These higher pressure areas are new reserves.

❏ Exploration is being conducted using 3-D seismic, which has been used to discover other producing formations below the existing fields. Hopefully, this trend will continue but the exact impact on helium extraction will probably be minimal. The discoveries are not expected to have tremendous natural gas reserves and the helium content is uncertain. The decline of the Kansas Hugoton and Panoma Fields will be extremely difficult to counteract, but any amount of new helium extraction will be helpful.

Current Helium Business

Historical production and extraction of helium in the United States is shown in Figure 5. The figure indicates a steady growth in helium recovered and sold since 1971, with greater percentage increases from 1986 to 1988, and smaller growth

from 1988 to 1992. Domestic helium sales were affected by the Algerian helium plant coming online around 1994. This is where the figure shows a decline in sales. The growth increased dramatically in late 1986 when Exxon Corporation began extraction of helium from Riley Ridge Field, Wyoming, at their Shute Creek plant. The extraction capability of this plant was recently increased from approximately 1.2 Bcf to 1.4 Bcf of pure helium per year, with the addition of a helium liquifier. Most of the growth in helium recovery since 1986 has been from the midcontinent area extraction plants. These plants sold about 900 MMcf of helium in 1987; in 2000, they sold about 3,100 MMcf of helium, which computes to an average annual growth of approximately 10 percent.

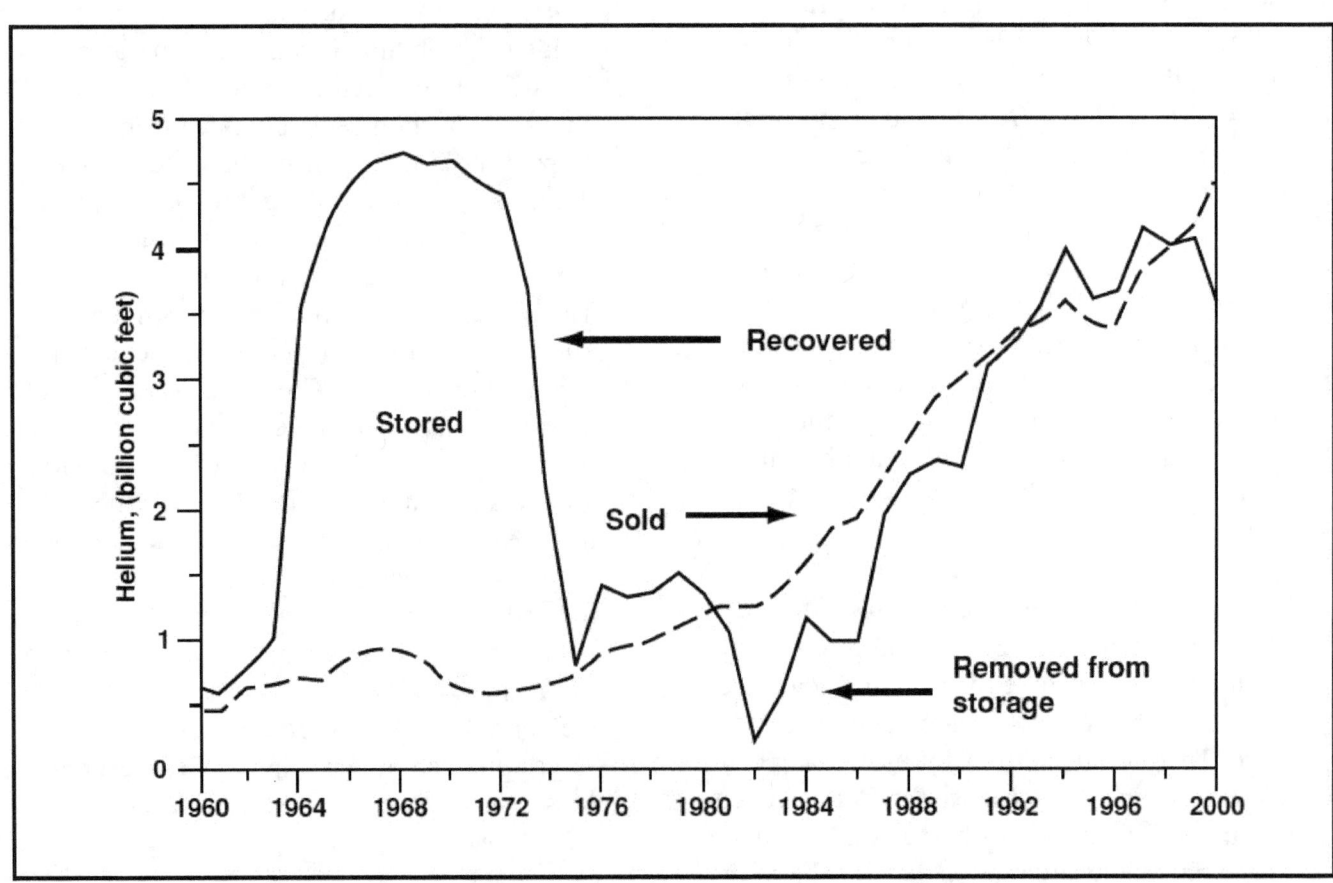

Figure 5. Historical production and extraction of helium in the United States.

Figure 6 shows the impact of sales and declining crude helium extraction in the midcontinent area on the Cliffside Gasfield. The area between the sales and production lines on a year-by-year basis is the estimated withdrawal from Cliffside storage to meet demand. Riley Ridge area helium production and extraction was not included in this projection because helium extraction at the Shute Creek plant is near capacity, excluding any additional plant changes, which would allow for greater plant gas throughput. The pure helium plant capacity in the midcontinent has been increased since the last report. The helium purification capacity of plants connected to the Cliffside Gasfield via the Government's conservation pipeline has increased from about 3.4 to 4 Bcf, annually.

The helium production curve is based on the projected decline of gas from the helium-rich natural gasfields in Kansas, Oklahoma, and Texas. These fields include Bradshaw, Greenwood, Kansas Hugoton, and Panoma Fields in Kansas; Guymon-Hugoton and Keyes in Oklahoma; and West Panhandle and Texas Hugoton in Texas. The possible decline of helium sales through technological advances or extraction of helium outside the United States may play a major role in the future of the helium industry. The growth in sales of United States produced helium in 2000 increased 12 percent compared to 1999 sales (15).

Presently, it is estimated that the extraction of helium from natural gas in the midcontinent area is from 70 to 75 percent of the total annual available helium. This represents the helium recovered at the crude helium plants. Some of the gathered natural gas is used to run compression

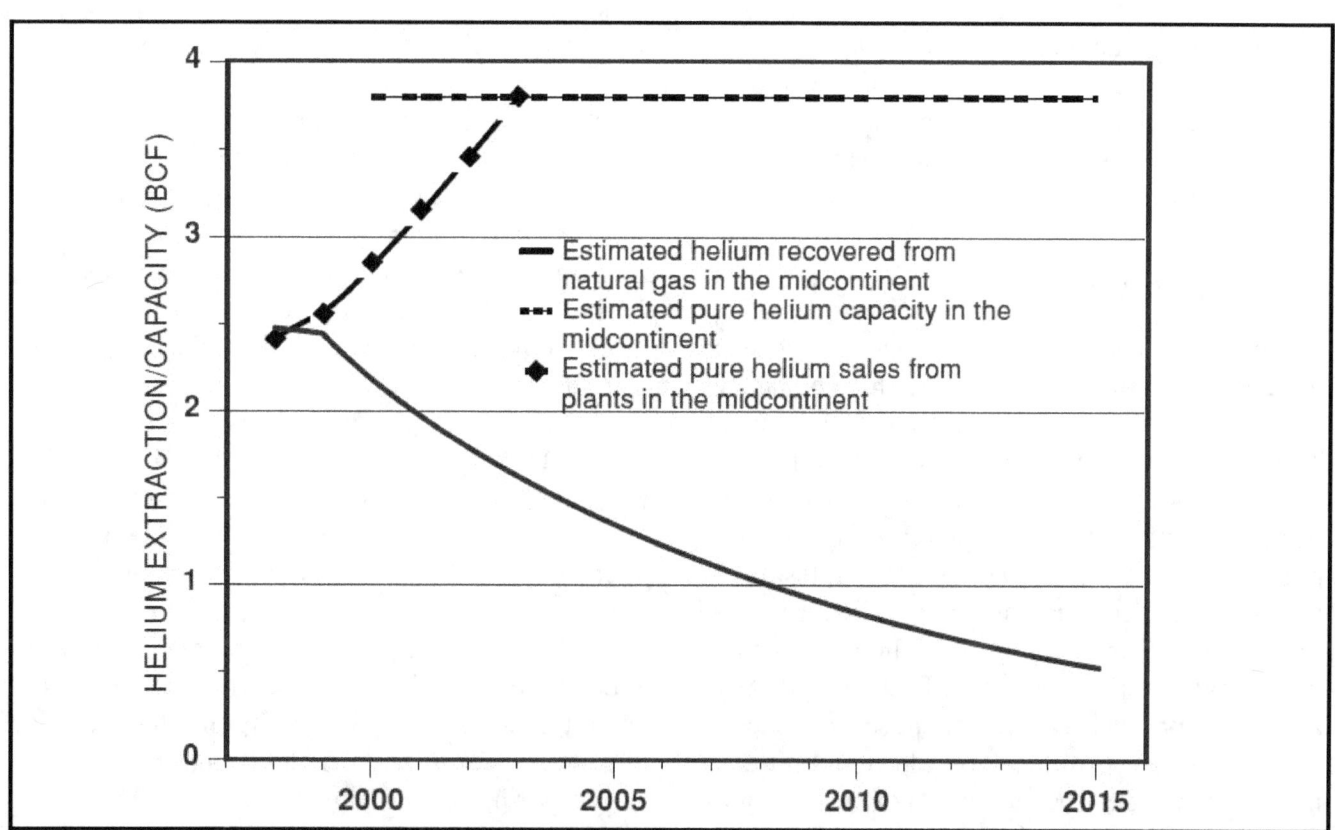

Figure 6. The impact of sales and declining crude helium extraction in the midcontinent area on the Cliffside Gasfield.

with the helium contained in that natural gas lost to the atmosphere. Also, some helium is lost at the crude helium and pure plants. These losses are estimated to be 10 to 15 percent, excluding any possible gathering system losses. The addition of compression will burn more natural gas and thus losses of helium will increase if the gathered natural gas continues to be used as fuel for compression.

Crude helium plants in the midcontinent have an extraction capacity of about 3 Bcf per year. However, only about 2.1 Bcf of this capacity was utilized during 2000. One crude helium plant is currently not extracting helium, and there is no change expected in this status for at least a year, possibly in 2002. This results in an annual loss of produced crude helium of about 400 MMcf. Private industry withdrew a net amount of 1,013 MMcf of helium from the Cliffside Gasfield during 2000. The withdrawal of helium from the Cliffside Gasfield in 2001 is expected to exceed 1 Bcf, and it is conceivable that it could be around 1.5 Bcf. The withdrawal of helium started in 1999 when about 113 MMcf of helium was produced from Cliffside.

Explanation of Figure 6

The graph presented in this report has been changed to depict the estimated helium that may be taken from the Cliffside Gasfield to meet helium demand. The field is expected to be in withdrawal mode for the immediate future, and it is likely that this trend will continue. The graph represents a simplistic view of the actual pure helium sales that are to be expected. The actual pure helium sales and crude helium extraction will not follow a straight line, but will be a jagged curve. This is based on several factors such as pure helium sale declines or increases, plant problems, or additional pure helium extraction. The production of crude helium from the Cliffside Gasfield is impacted by any of the previous factors and other changes that were not addressed.

The assumptions made in the graph are based on information obtained from private industry. This will not reflect the exact data going into the future, but is meant to be used as a guide to persons interested in the future of the helium market. The estimated versus actual data will fluctuate on a year-to-year basis. For instance, the helium estimated to be withdrawn from the Cliffside Gasfield during 2000 was about 0.7 Bcf on the graph, but actual demand was 1.019 Bcf.

The private pure helium plants connected to the Cliffside Gasfield via the Government's conservation pipeline have a combined nameplate capacity of about 4 Bcf. However, it is expected that the actual helium extraction capability is closer to 3.8 Bcf, excluding any additional capacity being added in the future. The point at which the sales of pure helium intersect the capacity of the pure helium plants means that other sources of helium must be found to take up any additional growth in helium demand.

The crude-helium production depicted on the graph is the estimated annual helium to be extracted from natural gas in the midcontinent area. The crude-helium extracted as a percentage of helium available was escalated from the current extraction of 70–75 percent to 90 percent over the time period covered. This would mean that all helium would be extracted, with the losses taken at the compressors and the plants. This may be unrealistic today and more so in the future since additional compression is expected to be added in the area. The decline of the available crude helium recovered from natural gas in the midcontinent is set at 10 percent over the time period. This was close to a mid-range value of the decline rates received from well operators, which were for the Hugoton and Panoma Fields. Taking into account the decline rates of other fields and the added capacity for crude helium extraction, 10 percent was chosen as the decline rate. The Kansas Corporation Commission has recently allowed operators, upon request, to pull vacuum on wells in the Hugoton area. At the time of this report, there were not many wells that had gone to vacuum. The rate of decline of production will be greater than 10 percent in the future. The data presented in the graph may be optimistic, which would mean that the Cliffside Gasfield would be utilized even more than depicted on the graph.

The portion of helium shown between the estimated helium recovered from natural gas in the midcontinent and the estimated pure helium sales from plants in the midcontinent is estimated to be the production from the Cliffside Gasfield. Based on the current rate of withdrawal of private helium, it is estimated that the private crude helium storage could be depleted as soon as mid-year 2003. This does not allow for the fact that some storage contract holders have more helium stored in the Cliffside Gasfield than others. This may mean that there will be some shortfalls based on individual private company crude-helium storage being exhausted prior to mid-year 2003. The effects of this may be related to some extent to future helium regulations to allow for the sale of Government crude helium on the open market. This is to be done no later than January, 1, 2005, as stated in the Helium Privatization Act of 1996. Also, at the current rate, the Government's stockpile of crude-helium could be depleted by 2015. The development of other helium extraction may lengthen the time to depletion of the Cliffside Gasfield crude helium.

Summary

This report uses several criteria to determine reserves, marginal reserves, and subeconomic resources, including helium content, proximity to major gas transmission lines, and size of field. Refinements in evaluating the helium reserves have been made in this report to represent actual estimated reserves being depleted to meet helium demand. In previous Bureau reports, it was concluded that relatively large volumes of helium would be available from natural gas through 2020, although that helium would probably be in gases with leaner concentrations than those being processed today. This report does not estimate nationwide projections for helium in natural gas production. Rather, the report focuses on short-term supply and demand for helium and examines the possible need for helium, with focus on the Cliffside Gasfield. Figure 6 is used to project the possible need for helium to be delivered from Cliffside Gasfield, and to show the need for additional helium extraction capabilities.

The Cliffside Gasfield has played a vital role in helping to supply the worldwide helium demand, especially during the year 2000. The withdrawal of private storage from the Cliffside Gasfield not only has to meet worldwide helium growth, but also is counted on to make up for declines of helium available to be extracted from the natural gas in the midcontinent. The near term most probable source of helium is the Government's helium supply being sold on the open market. However, according to the Helium Privatization Act of 1996, crude helium from the Government's reserve will be offered for sale on a straight-line basis and is likely to fall short of demand. The planned projects are not expected to initiate production prior to 2004, and a worldwide shortage of helium could occur. Any helium required to meet the demand for helium will come from the Cliffside Gasfield in the near term.

As of December 31, 2000, there are 33.7 Bcf of helium stored in Bush Dome at Cliffside Gasfield. The Bureau owns 29.6 Bcf and 4.1 Bcf is owned by private companies. There are also approximately 3.7 Bcf of helium contained in the natural gas in Bush Dome. The present trend is toward withdrawal of helium from Cliffside Gasfield to meet demand. The helium stored by the Government is set to be sold starting no later than January 1, 2005, with proceeds to be used to pay the helium debt. This is in compliance with the Helium Privatization Act of 1996.

There are nondepleting helium resources throughout the United States that will act to conserve helium; however, several factors will need to be considered prior to production of this gas. Some of the factors are: 1) the location of the field(s), 2) the helium resources of the field(s), 3) the economics of helium extraction from the natural gas stream of the field(s), and 4) field(s) located on Federal lands may be restricted by regulations from processing the gas stream for the sole purpose of helium extraction. Helium regulations are in the process of being developed and will be published for comments in the Federal Register.

Additional helium extraction outside of the mid-continent area is needed now to meet demand and to conserve a valuable resource.

References

1. Moore, B.J. 1976. Helium Resources of the United States, 1973. BuMines IC8708. 17pp.

2. ___.1979. Helium Resources of the United States, 1977. BuMines IC8803. 25pp.

3. ___.1979. Helium Resources of the United States, 1979. BuMines IC8831. 27 pp.

4. Hertweck, F.R., Jr. and R.D. Miller. 1983. Helium Resources of the United States, 1981. BuMines IC 8927. 17 pp.

5. Miller, R.D. 1985. Helium Resources of the United States, 1983. BuMines IC9028. 17 pp.

6. ___.1987. Helium Resources of the United States, 1985. BuMines IC9130. 16 pp.

7. ___.1988. Helium Resources of the United States, 1987. BuMines IC9189. 17 pp.

8. Miller, R.D. and John E. Hamak. 1990. Helium Resources of the United States, 1989. BuMines IC 9267. 14 pp.

9. Hamak, J.E. and B.D. Gage. 1993. Helium Resources of the United States, 1991. BuMines IC 9342. 18 pp.

10. Hamak, J.E. and D.L. Driskill. 1995. Helium Resources of the United States, 1993. BuMines IC 9436. 18 pp.

11. Gage, B.D. and D.L. Driskill. 1998. Helium Resources of the United States, 1997, Technical Note 403. Bureau of Land Management. BLM/HE/ST-98/002+3700. 28 pp.

12. Potential Gas Committee. 2001. Potential Supply of Natural Gas in the United States (as of December 31, 2000). Potential Gas Agency, Colorado Sch. Mines, Golden, Colorado. 346 pp.

13. Department of Energy, Energy Information Administration. 2000. U.S. Crude Oil, Natural Gas, and Natural Gas Liquids Reserves. 1996 Annual Report. DOE/EIA-0216(99). 156 pp.

14. Tongish, Claude A. 1980. Helium - Its Relationship to Geologic Systems and its Occurrence with the Natural Gases, Nitrogen, Carbon Dioxide, and Argon. BuMines RI8444. 176pp.

15. Pacheco, Norbert. 2001. Helium. 2000 Annual Report. United States Geological Survey, Reston, Virginia. 8pp.

Bibliography

Anderson, C.C. and H.H. Hinson. 1951. Helium-Bearing Natural Gases of the United States. Analyses and Analytical Methods. BuMines 486. 141pp.

Boone, W.J., Jr. 1958. Helium-Bearing Natural Gases of the United States. Analyses and Analytical Methods. Supplement to Bulletin 486. BuMines 576. 117pp.

Bureau of Land Management, Helium Operations. 1998. Analyses of Natural Gases, 1917-95. CD-ROM. NTIS PB 97-502611.

Cardwell, L.E. and L.F. Benton. 1970. Analyses of Natural Gases of the United States, 1968. BuMines IC8443. 169pp.

___. 1970. Analyses of Natural Gases, 1969. BuMines IC8475. 1970, 134pp.

___. 1971. Analyses of Natural Gases, 1970. BuMines IC8518. 130pp.

___. 1972. Analyses of Natural Gases, 1971. BuMines IC8554. 163pp.

___. 1973. Analyses of Natural Gases, 1972. BuMines IC8607. 104pp.

Gage, B.D. and D.L. Driskill. 1998. Analyses of Natural Gases, 1996-97, Technical Note 404. Bureau of Land Management. BLM/HE/ST 98/003+3700. 71 pp.

Hamak, J.E. and S. Sigler. 1989. Analyses of Natural Gases, 1988. BuMines IC9225. 66pp.

___. 1990. Analyses of Natural Gases, 1989. BuMines IC9256. 61pp.

___. 1991. Analyses of Natural Gases, 1990. BuMines IC9290. 56pp.

___. 1991. Analyses of Natural Gases, 1986-90. BuMines IC9301. 315pp.

Hamak, J.E. and B.D. Gage. 1992. Analyses of Natural Gases, 1991. BuMines IC9318. 97pp.

Hamak, J.E. and S. Sigler. 1993. Analyses of Natural Gases, 1992. BuMines IC9356. 62pp.

Hamak, J.E. and D.L. Driskill. 1996. Analyses of Natural Gases, 1994-95, Technical Note 399. Bureau of Land Management. BLM/HE/ST 97/002+3700. 68 pp.

Hertweck, F.R., Jr. and R.D. Miller. 1983. Helium Resources of the United States, 1981. BuMines IC8927. 17pp.

Hertweck, F.R., Jr. and D.D. Fox. 1984. Analyses of Natural Gases, 1983. BuMines IC8993. 127pp.

Miller, R.D. and G.P. Norrell. 1964. Analyses of Natural Gases of the United States, 1961. BuMines IC 8221. 148pp.

___. 1964. Analyses of Natural Gases of the United States, 1962. BuMines IC8239. 120pp.

___. 1965. Analyses of Natural Gases of the United States, 1963. BuMines IC8241. 102pp.

Miller, R.D. 1985. Helium Resources of the United States, 1983. BuMines IC9028. 17pp.

Miller, R.D. and F.R. Hertweck, Jr. Analyses of Natural Gases, 1981. BuMines IC8890, 1982, 84pp.

___. 1983. Analyses of Natural Gases, 1982. BuMines IC8942. 100pp.

Moore, B.J. 1974. Analyses of Natural Gases, 1973. BuMines IC8658. 96pp.

___. 1975. Analyses of Natural Gases, 1974. BuMines IC8684. 122pp.

___. 1976. Analyses of Natural Gases, 1917-74. BuMines Computer Printout. NTIS PB 251 202/AS. 889pp.

___. 1976. Helium Resources of the United States, 1973. BuMines IC8708. 17pp.

___. 1976. Analyses of Natural Gases, 1975. BuMines IC8717. 82pp.

___. 1977. Analyses of Natural Gases, 1976. BuMines IC8749. 94pp.

___. 1978. Analyses of Natural Gases, 1977. BuMines IC8780. 95pp.

___. 1979. Analyses of Natural Gases, 1978. BuMines IC8810. 113pp.

___. 1979. Helium Resources of the United States, 1977. BuMines IC8803. 25pp.

___. 1980. Analyses of Natural Gases, 1979. BuMines IC8833. 100pp.

___. 1980. Helium Resources of the United States, 1979. BuMines IC8831. 27pp.

___. 1981. Analyses of Natural Gases, 1980. BuMines IC8856. 236pp.

___. 1982. Analyses of Natural Gases, 1917-80. BuMines IC8870. 1,055pp.

Moore, B.J. and J.E. Hamak. 1985. Analyses of Natural Gases, 1984. BuMines IC9046. 102pp.

Moore. B.J., R.D. Miller, and R.D. Shrewsbury. 1966. Analyses of Natural Gases of the United States, 1964. BuMines IC8302. 144pp.

___. 1966. Analyses of Natural Gases of the United States, 1965. BuMines IC8316. 181pp.

___. 1967. Analyses of Natural Gases, 1966. BuMines IC8356. 130pp.

___. 1968. Analyses of Natural Gases of the United States, 1967. BuMines IC8395. 187pp.

Moore, B.J. and S. Sigler. 1985. Analyses of Natural Gases, 1985. BuMines IC9096. 182pp.

___. 1987. Analyses of Natural Gases, 1917-85. BuMines IC9129. 1,197pp.

___. 1987. Analyses of Natural Gases, 1986. BuMines IC9167. 101pp.

___. 1988. Analyses of Natural Gases, 1987. BuMines IC9188. 74pp.

Munnerlyn, R.D. and R.D. Miller. 1963. Helium-Bearing Natural Gases of the United States: Analyses. Second Supplement to Bulletin 486. BuMines 617. 93pp.

Sigler, S.M. 1994. Analyses of Natural Gases, 1993. BuMines IC9400. 58pp.

Glossary of Reserve and Resource Terms

The following definitions are based on definitions found in *Principles of a Resource/Reserve Classification of Minerals, Geological Survey Circular 831, 1980,* with additions and revisions where necessary to accommodate for helium.

Demonstrated - A term for the sum of measured and indicated.

Identified Resources - Resources whose location, grade, quality, and quantity are known or estimated from specific geologic evidence. Identified Resources include reserves, marginal reserves, and subeconomic resources components. To reflect varying degrees of geologic certainty, these economic divisions can be subdivided into measured, indicated, and inferred.[1]

Indicated - Quantity and quality are computed from information similar to that used for measured resources, but the amounts are less certain and can be estimated with a degree of certainty sufficient to indicate they are more likely to be recovered than not. In general, they include reserves in formations that appear to be productive based on log characteristics but that lack core data or definitive tests, and reserves that will be found by field extensions, in-fill drilling, or improved recovery methods.

Inferred - Estimates are based on an assumed continuity beyond measured and/or indicated resources, for which there is geologic evidence. Inferred resources may or may not be supported by analyses or measurements.

Inferred Reserve Base - The in-place part of an identified resource from which inferred reserves, marginal reserves, and subeconomic resources are estimated. Quantitative estimates are based largely on knowledge of the geologic character of a reservoir and for which there may be no gas analyses or measurements.

Marginal Reserves - That part of the reserve base which, at the time of determination, borders on being economically producible. Its essential characteristic is economic uncertainty. Included are resources that would be producible, given postulated changes in economic or technologic factors.

Measured - The quantity is computed from dimensions revealed by actual gas analyses; production or formation tests, electric logs, and core analyses; and/or delineated by drilling and defined by fluid contacts or undrilled areas that can be reasonably judged as commercially productive on the basis of geologic and engineering data.

---

[1]The terms *proved, probable,* and *possible,* which are commonly used by industry in economic evaluations of ore or mineral fuels in specific deposits, reservoirs, or districts, have been loosely interchanged with the terms *measured, indicated,* and *inferred.* The former terms are not a part of this classification system.

27

Other Occurrences - Resources which are contained in extremely low helium content natural gases or nonconventional natural gas reserves. Only "proved" and "probable" natural gas reserves of this type are evaluated and included in the classification.

Reserves - That part of the reserve base which is economically extracted or produced at the time of determination. The term reserves as used in this report is for fields from which helium is being extracted from the gas stream. Reserves include only recoverable materials; thus, terms such as "extractable reserves" and "recoverable reserves" are redundant and are not a part of this classification system.

Reserve Base - That part of an identified resource that meets specified minimum physical and chemical criteria related to current drilling and production practices, including those for quality, porosity, permeability, thickness, and depth. The reserve base is the in-place demonstrated resource from which reserves are estimated. It may encompass those parts of the resources that have a reasonable potential for becoming economically available within planning horizons beyond those that assume proven technology and current economics. The reserve base includes those resources that are currently considered reserves, marginal reserves, and some of those considered subeconomic resources. For helium, the measured portion of subeconomic resources is included in the reserve base but not the indicated portion.

Resource - A concentration of naturally occurring solid, liquid, or gaseous material in or on the earth's crust in such form and amount that economic extraction of a commodity from the concentration is currently or potentially feasible.

Subeconomic Resources - The part of identified resources that does not meet the economic criteria of reserves and marginal reserves.

Undiscovered Resources - Resources, the existence of which are only postulated, comprising deposits that are separate from identified resources. The undiscovered resources of helium are postulated based on the "speculative" resources reported by the Potential Gas Committee (PGC).

APPENDIX A
Guidelines for Determining Helium Reserves and Resources

The following guidelines apply for determining helium reserves, marginal helium reserves, and subeconomic helium resources as contained in this publication. The guidelines also are helpful for determining undiscovered resources.

Individual Field Reserves and Resources

Helium Content %	Contained Helium in Field/Area	Category
		Reserves*
≥0.30	150 MMcf - 1 Bcf	Marginal Reserves
≥0.30	10 - 150 MMcf	Subeconomic Resources
0.10 - 0.30	1 - 5 Bcf	Subeconomic Resources
0.10 - 0.30	150 MMcf - 1 Bcf	Subeconomic Resources
0.10 - 0.30	10 - 150MMcf	Other Occurrences
0.05 - 0.10	≥5 Bcf	Subeconomic Resources
0.05 - 0.10	10 MMcf - 5 Bcf	Other Occurrences
<0.05	Large coalbed methane or carbon dioxide resources, >5 Bcf contained helium	Other Occurrences

The previous guidelines also apply for areawide classifications. In addition, the following guidelines are applied to basinwide resources. An average helium content is used for each basin and the reserves/resources determined by applying the average helium content to the basin's gas resource estimate for probable and possible categories. For the undiscovered resources, the average helium content is applied to minimum most likely and maximum speculative Potential Gas Committee (PGC) gas resource numbers.

Areawide Classifications

< 0.05	All DOE/EIA reserves after subtracting computerized data base measured reserves	Other Occurrences
<0.05	PGC probable gas resources in a basin or region.	Other Occurrences
ALL	PGC possible gas resources in a basin or region.	Subeconomic ** Resources

* Extraction is taking place from the fields and formations that are being produced. Therefore, there is no need for a designation based on helium content of the natural gas.

** The move from Marginal Reserves to Subeconomic Resources was made based on the determination that extraction of helium from these sources is not likely.

REPORT DOCUMENTATION PAGE

1. AGENCY USE ONLY (Leave blank)	2. REPORT DATE	3. REPORT TYPE AND DATES COVERED
	December 2001	Final

4. TITLE AND SUBTITLE

Helium Resources of the United States–2001

5. FUNDING NUMBERS

6. AUTHOR(S)

Brent D. Gage and David L. Driskill

7. PERFORMING ORGANIZATION NAME(S) AND ADDRESS(ES)

U.S. Department of the Interior
Bureau of Land Management
Denver Federal Center
Bldg. 50, ST-150
Denver, CO 80225-0047

8. PERFORMING ORGANIZATION REPORT NUMBER

BLM/NM/ST-02/001+3700

9. SPONSORING/MONITORING AGENCY NAME(S) AND ADDRESS(ES)

10. SPONSORING/MONITORING AGENCY REPORT NUMBER

11. SUPPLEMENTARY NOTES

12a. DISTRIBUTION/AVAILABILITY STATEMENT

12b. DISTRIBUTION CODE

13. ABSTRACT (Maximum 200 words)

This report differs from past reports in defining helium reserves in that it includes only the estimated helium contained in fields and formations from which helium is currently being recovered. Previous reports had placed nondepleting fields and formations into the helium reserve category.

The identified helium resources of the United States are estimated at 468 Bcf, as of December 31, 2000. This includes 144 Bcf of demonstrated reserves, 137 Bcf of demonstrated marginal reserves, and 37 Bcf of demonstrated subeconomic resources. The identified resources also include 150Bcf of helium in inferred subeconomic resources. The demonstrated helium resources contained on Federal lands are approximately 155 Bcf, including 30 Bcf in underground storage in the Cliffside Gasfield near Amarillo, Texas. In addition to the identified helium resources, undiscovered helium resources in the United States are estimated at a most likely volume of 110 Bcf, with a maximum volume of 254Bcf and a minimum volume of 45 Bcf. Also reported are 53 Bcf of helium in nonconventional and low helium content natural gases.

Current extraction of helium in the United States occurs mainly from natural gases produced from the Hugoton gas area in Kansas, Oklahoma, and Texas, and the Riley Ridge area in southwestern Wyoming. Helium sales in the United States in 2000 was approximately 4.5 Bcf, with 3.5 Bcf extracted from natural gas and 1.0 Bcf from crude helium storage at the Cliffside Gasfield. The volume of helium produced with the natural gas in the Hugoton area continues to decline. The current trend at the Cliffside Gasfield is the withdrawal of privately owned crude helium by private industry.

The growth of helium sales was about 330 MMcf from 1999 to 2000. This trend is expected to continue over the next 3 to 4 years with exploitation of other sources of helium expected in 2004 and 2005. The pure plants currently located along the Government's pipeline will reach maximum helium production capacity at about this time. If the growth of sales continues to increase at about 300 MMcf per year and helium extraction from natural gas in the midcontinent declines at 10 percent annually, the expected helium projects will help slow the growth of withdrawal from the Cliffside Gasfield.

14. SUBJECT TERMS

Helium resources, demonstrated reserves, demonstrated marginal reserves, undiscovered helium resources, demonstrated subeconomic resources, crude helium plants, inferred reserves, inferred marginal reserves, inferred subeconomic resources

15. NUMBER OF PAGES

40 including covers

16. PRICE CODE

17. SECURITY CLASSIFICATION OF REPORT	18. SECURITY CLASSIFICATION OF THIS PAGE	19. SECURITY CLASSIFICATION OF ABSTRACT	20. LIMITATION OF ABSTRACT
Unclassified	Unclassified	Unclassified	UL